Anne Frank:
An Enduring Legacy

First published in 1999
Yes! Publications
10-12 Bishop St.
Derry BT48 6PW

Tel: (01504) 261941
Fax: (01504) 263700
E mail: yes.pubs@business.ntl.com

All rights reserved. No part of this book may be reprinted or reproduced or utilised in any electronic, mechanical, or other means, not known or hereafter invented, including photocopying or recording or otherwise, without the prior written permission of the publisher.

Copyright © 1999
Carol Rittner, R.S.M.

ISBN 1 873832 05 2

Cover Design: Julie Bowen
Typesetting: Hugh Gallagher
                Fionnuala Deane

Printed in Northern Ireland by Coleraine Printing Company.

Anne Frank
An Enduring Legacy

Edited by
Carol Rittner, R.S.M.

YES! Publications
Derry, Northern Ireland

For
Deirdre Mullan

"A friend is, as it were, a second self"

Contents

Introduction

Carol Rittner, R.S.M.: *Anne Frank: An Enduring Legacy*   1

Part One
ANNE FRANK IN THE WORLD

Dan Bar-on: *Why is Anne Frank's Diary So Important?*   5
Dermot Keogh: *Ireland and Northern Ireland During the Holocaust*   8
Victoria Barnett: *What and Who is a Bystander?*   11

Part Two
ANNE FRANK IN NORTHERN IRELAND

Johnston McMaster: *Foundations of Chaos or Peace?*   14
Deirdre Mullan: *Whispers of Hope from an Amsterdam Attic*   18
Richard Collins: *Standing at the Cross-roads*   21

Part Three
ANNE FRANK IN THE CLASSROOM

G. Jan Colijn: *Why Holocaust Studies?*   25
Leo Lieberman: *Anne Frank in the Classroom*   29
Mary Murphy: *Lesson Ongoing!*   33
Mary Johnston: *Anne Frank: A History for Today*   36

Resources for Teaching   40

INTRODUCTION

Anne Frank:
An Enduring Legacy

Carol Rittner, R.S.M.

Does the diary of Anne Frank, the young Jewish girl hidden in an Amsterdam attic for more than two years during the Nazi occupation of Holland, offer false hope in the face of the Holocaust's bottomless horror? Cynthia Ozick, the American Jewish writer thinks it does. In fact, in an essay published in *The New Yorker* magazine, she suggests that it would have been better for the world if Anne's diary had been destroyed. While I do not agree with Ozick, I do think she is right to draw attention to what Jonathan Rosen calls Anne Frank's "untamed posthumous power." It is just such "posthumous power" Dan Bar-on examines in his contribution to this book, "Why is Anne Frank's Diary So Important?"

The *Diary of Anne Frank* is important, and no doubt will continue to be important for many years to come. People all over the world have read Anne's diary, and millions more will read it, in and out of school. Young people will continue to get caught up in Anne's life in hiding because she describes so well her teenage "trials and tribulations," which resonate with their own. While the unfathomable darkness surrounding Anne and the other inhabitants in the Secret Annex never dominates the pages of her diary, neither is it totally absent. She writes not only about her hopes and expectations but about her fears as well.

Anne did not leave us a record of the horrible experiences she endured after she and the other "Secret Annexers" were betrayed, arrested by SS *Oberscharfuhrer*, Karl Josef Silberbauer and three Dutch policemen, then sent with other Dutch Jews to the East in the late Summer of 1944, but we do have witness accounts from others about what happened in the Nazi death camps: Gisela Perl, Olga Lengyl, Victor Frankl, Primo Levi, and Elie Wiesel, to name but a few. If we are tempted to forgot the grisly murder of six million Jews during the Holocaust, Perl, Lengyl, Frankl, Levi, and Wiesel are there to remind us that Anne Frank's story does not end on the last page of her diary.

Like so many nameless and faceless Jews during the Holocaust, Anne probably died a horrible death – emaciated, covered with sores, and naked, perhaps even despairing of "God and man." Such an image should temper our tendency to romanticise Anne Frank as the eternal image of optimistic and defiant survival she has become for so many.

The *Diary of Anne Frank* has a historical context – World War II and the Holocaust – and we should study and teach about it within that context, but we should do so in a way that also encourages us to examine its legacy for today.

Marjorie Agosin, born in Chile, now resident in America and teaching at Wellesley College, does just that in her essay, "Anne Frank, or the Landscape Uprooted":

> Anne Frank's diary makes us re-evaluate the relationship among the everyday present, the past, and the concept of nationhood. The Netherlands was one country that openly declared its solidarity with its Jewish citizens, but even so, a great number were murdered, in part because the flat openness and easy accessibility of the landscape did not permit safely hiding them.
>
> Must nations possess a confounding geography in order to save human life? What must the moral fabrics of nations be like if they are to avoid holocausts and genocide? What is it that causes people to refuse to obey the forces of demagoguery? The diary makes us think concretely about our relationship with national identity and landscape. Nearly all of Europe obeyed the German call, with only a small minority of European countries hiding and protecting Jews, thus giving rein to the systematic extermination of six-million Jews.

> Anne Frank was banished and condemned by a collective amnesia of silence and terror. During the transfer of victims to death camps, people stood by silently and watched, distant and removed onlookers, as if the gasping bodies of the victims marked off zones of the unspeakable and unimaginable. Anne Frank's diary confronts us with history's transformations and postulates the human tragedy of nationalism and the contemptible legacy of racism that today remain powerful weapons to divide people and lead them down hatred's path.

In remembering the Jewish teenager Anne Frank, as well as all the victims of the Nazis during World War II and the Holocaust, we should remember that before the first shot of war, or before the first persecution and murder of an innocent victim by a fascist government, movement, or individual, there are daily acts of violence, large and small, and countless vehement words which cumulatively make the taking of human life seem not only normal but also necessary. Categories of contempt serve to designate other human beings as "the enemy" or "inhuman."

All categories of contempt are exceedingly dangerous and help to create an atmosphere in which violence is not only possible but almost inevitable. It is imperative that all of us, but especially those in positions of leadership – political, religious, social, and intellectual – clearly and unequivocally condemn all forms of contempt and every type of violent rhetoric which excludes anyone from our universe of moral concern. And that we must do it immediately, at the beginning, before the avalanche begins.

What does it take for us human beings to remain life-size in a time of moral diminishment? Perhaps such a question is one of the enduring legacies of the *Diary of Anne Frank*. If it's not, I think it ought to be.

The essays that follow, try to respond to the question, "What does Anne Frank have to say to us today?" Most of the authors are themselves teachers, either in high school or university. All are concerned about education, whether as parents or teachers. Their intent in writing these essays was to provide their colleagues with some ideas and suggestions that might prove helpful when teaching the *Diary of Anne Frank* or preparing students for a visit to the exhibition.

I want to thank everyone who contributed to *Anne Frank: An Enduring Legacy*. All did so in the midst of many other professional and personal obligations, and so I am deeply grateful to everyone for once again responding to one of my many invitations to "write something" for me.

I also would like to thank Henry ("Hank") Klos, a student of mine at The Richard Stockton College of New Jersey, USA, who helped to compile the suggested "Teaching Resources" listed at the end of the book. In addition, I want to thank Julie Bowen in the Graphics Department at Stockton College and my other colleagues who were so helpful.

Fionnuala Deane and Hugh Gallagher, the "heart and soul" of Yes! Publications deserve not only my thanks for all they did to creatively design and publish *Anne Frank: An Enduring Legacy*, but my admiration for their generosity, professionalism, and good humour. Finally, my grateful thanks to Maureen Hetherington, Community Relations Officer, Derry City Council, Londonderry, Northern Ireland, for support and encouragement.

Carol Rittner, R.S.M., *Distinguished Professor of Religion at The Richard Stockton College of New Jersey, USA, is the editor of Anne Frank: An Enduring Legacy.*

Part One

ANNE FRANK IN THE WORLD

Why is Anne Frank's Diary So Important?

Dan Bar-On

Whenever one asks young people in Europe, Israel, or the United States which book they have read about the Holocaust, which they can recall, in nine out of ten cases they will refer to the *Diary of Anne Frank*. This was true 20 years ago and it is still true today. I have asked myself many times why young people recall especially this book? What makes this story so special that all over the world it fascinates young people's imagination more than any other book, theatre play, or movie which has been written or shown about the Holocaust? The house of Anne Frank in Amsterdam is one of the most visited museums in Europe, and so are the exhibitions, carrying her name, *Anne Frank in the World*, and *Anne Frank: A History for Today*, which continue to move around the Western world, visiting many cities, large and small.

I am sure there are many different answers to this question. First of all, we know that for young people one personal account is much more meaningful than figures or facts about millions of dead people who were murdered during the Holocaust. Second, Anne Frank was a young pretty girl who wrote a personal and very vivid diary. This is something which young people, especially young girls, can identify with. They can hear their own voice when she describes her relationships with her parents, with other family members, her sexual awakening, and her relations with Peter. Third, and related to that, Anne is not pure and unreachable; she is human, with her selfish feelings, struggling with her own evil. This again makes it much more real and understandable for young people who struggle with similar emotions and internal conflicts in their own lives. Fourth, the threat of evil, though it is somewhere in the background, does not take over the scenery in the Diary itself. We can hear the threatening voices behind the door, downstairs, in the street, but her family's hiding place was not broken into, at least, not until the very end. In most of the Diary, life goes on, more or less normally. There are fears and moments of high tension, but they do not overshadow the light and the vividness of her life.

This special combination, however, also has created an illusion. The illusion may lead young people to imagine to themselves that perhaps the story had a happy ending after all. If Anne is such a wonderful young girl, who would want to harm her? Perhaps, at some point some good angels came and rescued her. Otherwise, how could we hear her story today? Or, alternatively, those who wanted to harm her or her family were really very evil people. Such evil people are outside our imagination. Anne did not encounter them, therefore, we really should not bother too much about them. The encapsulated environment in which her diary has been displayed supports this illusion.

We can not really grasp what was going on outside her hiding place. We have been taken into it with her, and wish to stay there in order not to really know what at the same time was going on outside that attic. Young people, not less than Anne Frank herself, need some kind of a shelter from the cruel world which the Holocaust had created for her, for them, for all of us. Anne's story provides us with this shelter. We will stay with her in hiding until evil vanishes from the world, by itself. Once it vanishes, we shall be able to move back into the world and inhabitant it again, together with our lovely Anne.

By this analysis I do not intend to belittle the robust beauty of her story, or of her innocent soul. I am just trying to make sense of why and how so many young people may use her story as a way of trying to grasp something of what happened during the Holocaust, while at the same time keeping a reasonable distance from it.

It may still be our huge task to build on what her story has accomplished while at the same time trying to have students work through, at a later stage, some of this distance. Only by working through this distance will they become aware of the less pleasant parts of the Holocaust, and thereby perhaps also become protagonists for active prevention of future man-made calamities. More than the story of Anne Frank will be needed for this huge task, though her diary provides us with a good beginning on this long road.

Dan Bar-On is Professor of Psychology at Ben-Gurion University of the Negev, Beer Sheva, Israel, where he also is the Chair of a new Centre for Dialogue Between Populations in Conflict.

Ireland and Northern Ireland During the Holocaust

Dermot Keogh

The face of Anne Frank is universally recognisable; she personifies the tragedy of the Holocaust and is a symbol of what might have been. Hidden for most of the war in the annex of an Amsterdam house by very brave people, the Frank family was betrayed, discovered and transported to the death camps in 1944. Only Anne's father survived.

But what if she and many other Jewish families had been given refuge away from Nazi control in unoccupied Europe. The governments of Northern Ireland and of Ireland - situated in Belfast and Dublin respectively - were in a position to have acted more generously towards the many pleas from Jewish families for temporary shelter during the 1930s. Neither Eamon de Valera's neutral Ireland nor the government of Northern Ireland acted with magnanimity. The policy of both North and South was to keep the majority of the refugees out - and Jewish refugees in particular.

The files in the Public Record Office, Belfast, and in the National Archives, Dublin, show the reticence of both governments to let Jews "in." The Department of Justice in the South wrote in December 1945 that "the immigration of Jews is generally discouraged" and their officials had acted on that principle throughout the war. Why? What was the rationale of the author of that document which was sent to the cabinet? It was felt that Jews did not assimilate and that might create a social problem - a social problem which would be exacerbated by "the wealth and influence of the Jewish community in this country."

In Northern Ireland, officials in the relevant government departments did not make explicit their feelings about Jews - but very few were allowed in during the 1930s except when they were in a position to bring wealth and entrepreneurial expertise. According to the 1937 census, there were 1,472 Jews living there; 1,284 in Belfast. The vast majority of the community were the descendants of those refugees who had arrived in the 1880s and 1890s escaping the Russian pogroms. The growth of anti-Semitism on the continent of Europe in the 1930s did not add significantly to that number. However, the actions of the Belfast Jewish community did help save the lives of over 100 Jewish boys who lived and worked on a farm at Millisle, County Down.

The Dublin Jewish community also helped with the Millisle project and were active in trying to bring other Jewish refugees to southern Ireland. The Jewish population there was 3,907, divided mainly between the cities of Dublin and Cork. Descended mainly from Lithuanian Jews fleeing the Russian pogroms, the community failed to overturn the ungenerous refugee policy of the Irish government even if, on occasion, they had some individual successes.

Irish Jews lived for the first two years of the war under the fear of invasion. They had attempted, usually without much success in the 1930s, to encourage the Dublin authorities to allow Jews to take refuge in the country. Their efforts were not helped by the fact that the Irish envoy in Berlin, Charles Bewley, was a strong Nazi supporter. Given the scale of the refugee problem in the two years before the outbreak of war, Bewley had been given the freedom to make decisions on which application would be sent back to Dublin for processing. It is likely that his proven anti-Semitism conditioned him not to send home visa applications from Jewish families.

In that way, it is not known how many children like Anne Frank might have been saved had their visa applications been sent to Dublin for processing. After the war, the Taoiseach (Prime Minister) Eamon de Valera sought to liberalise Irish refugee policy and counteracted the bias against Jews which was evident in the Department of Justice. In 1948, a party of over 100 Jewish orphans were allowed to enter the country where they lived for about one year before leaving for permanent homes in Britain, Palestine, Canada and the United States.

Throughout the war, de Valera had remained in contact with his close friend, Isaac Herzog, who had been Chief Rabbi of the Irish Free State between 1920 and 1937, when he moved to Palestine. Herzog had intervened many times during those years and de Valera had responded positively. But wartime conditions prevented Jews from being allowed by the Nazi authorities to come to Ireland. In this area, de Valera acted independently of the Department of Justice. Having established a close working relationship with Jews in Ireland, de Valera astounded many of his supporters at home by visiting the German Minister to express his condolences on the death of Hitler in early May 1945. De Valera was not anti-Semitic. Irish Jews knew that. But his action caused them deep pain - as it did many other Irish citizens at home and abroad - and they remained very hurt.

Today the Jewish community in both parts of Ireland is very small - about 400 in Northern Ireland and less than 1,000 in the South. A commonly expressed view within the Jewish community is that history need not have been like that. Even a small number of Anne Franks would have helped strengthen the Jewish community at a critical time and prevent the decline which is now inevitable.

Dermot Keogh, *Professor of History at University College Cork, Republic of Ireland, is the author of* Jews in Twentieth Century Ireland – Refugees, anti-Semitism and the Holocaust *published by Cork University Press.*

What and Who is a Bystander?

Victoria Barnett

This essay is excerpted, with the author's permission, from Victoria Barnett's forthcoming book about Bystanders which will be published in 1999 by Greenwood Publications, USA.

The literature about the Holocaust is filled with bystanders. Whether the topic is Vichy France, the medical profession, the behaviour of Polish villagers or German soldiers, the issue of bystander behaviour arises. The term usually refers to someone immediately present, an actual witness, someone for whom involvement was an option. *It implies a certain form of behaviour.*

It also presupposes a certain detachment; bystanders are not automatically involved. The term "bystander" does not apply to leading Nazis or guards in concentration camps, but to "ordinary citizens." In some fashion, they simply went about their daily lives during one of the ghastliest dictatorships the world has ever known. They continued to work and raise their children. Those who lived near concentration camps tended their gardens and had regular dealings with those who worked and ran the camps. After November 9, 1938, when thousands of German stores previously owned by Jews suddenly had new owners, people continued to shop in them, as though nothing had changed.

They were people who, to their vast relief, were convinced after 1945 that they had not been directly involved in the genocide of the Jews. And, if we consider how the world must have looked to these people, they are not really that difficult to understand. People throughout the world adjust to their political circumstances. Most people are far more preoccupied with maintaining the normal rhythms of their lives than with the wish to become involved — perhaps at some risk — to alleviate the suffering of others.

Yet, in the post-Holocaust awareness that "normal" life was proceeding while millions of people were murdered, the bystander becomes an especially haunting figure. As the narrator of Wiesel's 1964 novel, *The Town Beyond the Wall*, says:

> This, this was the thing I had wanted to understand ever since the war. Nothing else. How a human being can remain indifferent. The executioners I understood; also the victims, though with more difficulty. For the others, all the others, those who were neither for nor against, those who sprawled in passive patience, those who told themselves, "The storm will blow over and everything will be normal again," those who thought themselves above the battle, those who were permanently and merely spectators — all those were closed to me, incomprehensible.[1]

How do we comprehend and judge such attitudes, in ourselves and in others? Our response to this question depends partly on our own judgements about the circumstances that bystanders faced. Did they have choices? Did they have the power to change what happened? Do dictatorships induce a kind of mass psychosis that transforms some people into brutes and others into passive marionettes? Were they ideologically conditioned, blinded by prejudice to the suffering of those who didn't belong to their religious or ethnic group? What factors move people to altruistic behaviour; what factors keep people passive? What is the nature of the sin we are addressing here political? moral? all too human? What does the Holocaust tell us about ourselves and God? *How, particularly within the Christian and Jewish traditions, do we wrestle with the questions it raises?*

As all these questions suggest, the bystanders are not just a historical phenomenon. They raise troubling questions about human nature and the very foundations of human ethics. If we decide that a Holocaust should never happen again, we must think about the behaviour of those who were present, but did nothing to stop the evil or help its victims.

Notes

1. Elie Wiesel, *The Town Beyond the Wall,* New York: Avon Books, 1969, 159.

***Victoria Barnett**, author of* For the Soul of the People, *published by Oxford University Press, is a consultant to the Church Relations Committee of the Holocaust Memorial Museum, Washington, DC, USA.*

Part Two

ANNE FRANK IN NORTHERN IRELAND

Foundations of Chaos or Peace?

Johnston McMaster

The twentieth century will go down in history as a century of incredible technological achievement. Yet it is also the most bloody in recorded human history. War and conflict claimed more lives than in any other century. Abuses of human rights have also been a major characteristic along with millions of deaths from poverty and hunger. There is a dark shadow side to the twentieth century. Humankind has the frightening capacity for inhumanity, indeed a brutality beyond rational explanation.

The Holocaust is one of the most terrible blotches in human history. Two years ago, when on a peace study visit to Israel/Palestine, I visited Yad Vashem, the Holocaust Memorial in Jerusalem. The international group walked around in silence. There were no words to be spoken. There were almost no thoughts possible, even feelings, when walking through the part of the Memorial commemorating the children who died in the death camps. Is this what human beings have the capacity to do to each other?

This terrible atrocity was against the Jewish people. The planned, systematic elimination of life by the Nazis also included Gypsies and homosexuals. Those who did not fit into the ideological dream, who were different, and who were perceived as threatening the purity of race and ideology were to be removed.

Anne Frank wrote in April 1944 that "We've been strongly reminded of the fact that we're Jews in chains, chained to the one spot, without any rights, but with a thousand obligations . . . The time will come when we'll be people again and not just Jews!"

Anti-Semitism has a long history. Rooted in prejudice, ignorance and fear, it has led to persecution and pogroms against the Jewish people. Modern Irish history is not free from it. It is also part of the mechanism of scapegoating. Some group must be demonised and held responsible for society's ills. It avoids facing up to responsibilities. "Jews in chains" is a way of not facing up to our collective failure; of transferring our prejudices and irrational fears; of preserving our identity myths. As we delude ourselves with dreams of ethnic, cultural or religious purity, error has no rights and those who do not fit become the targets of hatred and fear. They may even have to be eliminated to preserve the myth.

Women also suffer inequalities and discrimination in a hierarchical and patriarchal world. Writing on 13th June 1944, Anne is bothered as to "why women have been, and still are, thought to be so inferior to men." She presumes that men have dominated women from the very beginning. But women have the right to be completely independent and respected as well. "What I condemn are our system values and the men who don't acknowledge how great, difficult, but ultimately beautiful women's share in society is."

Gender inequality has not gone away. Patriarchal and dominating models of power still prevail. More needs to be done to create a meaningful equality agenda. Gender equality is one of the objectives of the 1998 Belfast Agreement and an essential part of any peace process.

Anne experienced shortage of food, and not just that, but the corruption of black market ration books. Those who supplied them with food coupons had been arrested. On the 14th March 1944, lunch consisted of mashed potatoes and pickled kale. "You wouldn't believe how much kale can stink when it's a few years old!" Then she mentions the inevitable diseases.

Basic human rights are denied and there is the spiral of suffering. Moral sensitivity is corrupted as a black market develops. Shortage of food and an unbalanced diet bring on disease. Human well-being collapses. And it is not just about economic factors. There is conflict and violence involved spawning a range of destructive problems.

People have the right to adequate food, water, a balanced diet, a roof over their head and to live in peace and security. Human rights are of fundamental importance. Deny them and a bloody harvest is reaped. Northern Ireland has had its own experience of that, though there are still those who deny any connection between unjust arrangements of power and the structural forms of discrimination, and the violent conflict that ensued. But seeds of injustice always reap the bitter harvest of violence.

"It's utterly impossible for me to build my life on a foundation of chaos, suffering and death." So wrote Anne on 15th July 1944. She had experienced intolerance, the denial of human rights, the violence of a corrupt system, the abuse of power and the lust for dominance. Chaos, suffering and death were the foundation and one which does not allow a human person anywhere to realise the full potential of his/her humanity. Anne feels "the suffering of millions." There is a solidarity with all those who suffer inhumanity.

All human persons need the space, and in relation to others, the opportunity to build their lives as dignified and worthwhile human persons. Every person's right is the right to live in a peaceful community. The Jewish word is "shalom," a word that encompasses the total well-being of the person within the total well-being of a community. Shalom is a community peace which is personal, social, economic and political. Anne dreams of such a peace.

"And yet, when I look up at the sky, I somehow feel that everything will change for the better, that this cruelty too will end, that peace and tranquillity will return once more. In the meantime, I hold on to my ideals. Perhaps the day will come when I'll be able to realise them."

The Nazi dream was exclusive and destructive. We need dreams of peace which are inclusive, large enough to embrace a rich, diverse and pluralistic society; where tolerance, compassion and justice for all are the core values; where people can realise their potential in responsible relationships and community.

Anne Frank held on to such ideals, even in the darkness. Such ideals, hopes and dreams are not "pie in the sky." They energise and empower us to actively work for their realisation. There is a future vision always breaking into the present.

Anne also looked for the day when they could be people, and "not just Jews!" In Northern Ireland, we too might live and relate as people, going beyond our distorting labels.

Johnston McMaster, *a Methodist minister, is Lecturer in Ecumenical Theology and Co-ordinator of Adult Education Programmes at the Irish School of Ecumenics in Belfast, Northern Ireland.*

Whispers of Hope from an Amsterdam Attic

Deirdre Mullan

She was thirteen when forced into hiding in a small attic at the back of a building in Amsterdam. She was outgoing, friendly, and fun loving. She wrote in her diary, "I have darling parents and a sister of sixteen. I know thirty people whom I might call friends. I don't seem to lack anything." Like most girls I teach, and like most girls her age, Anne Frank had many questions about life, but because her life was cut short, she never had a chance to answer those questions.

When Holland was occupied by Nazi Germany during World War II, many people, afraid for their lives, let things happen. Some collaborated with the Nazis, hoping for some personal benefit. Others did nothing. They were *just* bystanders. And yet, then as now, there are people prepared to risk everything to uphold all that is good and decent in human beings.

As this century of human genocide comes to a close, I find myself reflecting on one hundred years of history, on wars and conflicts among peoples who inhabit our world, on the fact that genocide seems more the norm than the exception. Sometimes, I think about the thin line that separates, Yes from no, Love from Hate, Peace from War.

Now and then, I think about Otto Frank, Anne's father. I can almost feel the struggle within him between fear and trust. I can almost feel his anxiety. Did he take a deep breath before he asked, "Miep, are you willing to help us?

Years later, when she was asked why she said "Yes," Miep Gies said, "I'm not a hero. There is nothing special about me. I only did what seemed necessary at the time." Still, that risk, that fraction of a second, that "Yes" made all the difference in the world.

Are you are wondering what the tragic circumstances of a Jewish family in an Amsterdam attic for more than two years during WW II and the Holocaust has to do with us in the North of Ireland? I wondered that too, until April 1994 when Thornhill College hosted the *Anne Frank in the World* exhibition. That's when we asked the question, "If Anne Frank had been your neighbour, would you have helped?"

That's when I knew what a Jewish family hidden in Amsterdam more than 50 years ago had to do with us living here in Northern Ireland. When I reflect on that exhibition, and on the deaths of 432 people who have died in "the troubles" since then, as well as on the making and shaping of the *Good Friday Agreement* of April 1998, I find myself drawn to the words of another teenager, 15-year old Aine, one of my students:

> If Anne Frank had been my neighbour, I hope I would have helped. The story of war and persecutions does not always teach us the right lessons, but like Anne Frank, I refuse to succumb to depression. I think what hurt the Frank family most was not the cruelty of the Nazis, but the silence of their "friends." Why do human beings feel the need to hurt and degrade each other? I think I know a little about how Anne Frank and her family felt. My Dad also had to go into hiding when I was six years old. My Mum used to pack small packages for him and tell us his children again and again not to say to anyone that we had visited our Dad. I did not understand then, and I don't really understand now, why my Dad was selected for this special treatment. I felt utterly bewildered and afraid, especially in the night.

Anne Frank and her story are important in Northern Ireland today. Her whispers of hope from that Amsterdam attic are still needed so that people can move beyond xenophobia ("Why are *those people* coming here?"), beyond slogans ("*Our people* first!") and beyond scapegoating ("Who do *they* think *they* are?")

Anne's diary is a reminder and a warning to all of us – in Ireland, Bosnia, South Africa, Rwanda – *wherever* there is conflict and violence. Until we take her story seriously, the horrors of history will continue to repeat themselves. We need to look deep within; we need to check our "temperature of tolerance." It is too cosy to blame *the other* for past misdeeds. We, too, must accept our own responsibility.

I think it would be easier if evil people were visible committing evil deeds because then we could separate *them* from *us*. But, the line dividing good from evil is very thin indeed. It cuts through the heart of every human being. And who among us is willing to destroy her own heart?

Anne Frank and her Diary are important tools for educators to use during what I believe is a *teachable moment* in Northern Ireland's history. If we can read it with an open mind and a feeling heart, perhaps we shall be able to find creative ways to engage with one another, create new ways to live reverently and in right relation with each other, resist the shadow of death, which is never far away from any of us.

What can Anne and her Diary help me to nurture in the students I teach every day?

- A sense of their own cultural identity,
- An appreciation of the diversity of cultures which exists on the island of Ireland,
- A positive attitude to responsible citizenship within the European Community,
- A respect for people of other races, traditions and creeds,
- A belief that people "really are good at heart."

In a society where we are so vocal about rights, the real test of human decency is our willingness to assert the human rights of others, especially those who are different from us in one way or another.

Deirdre Mullan, *a Sister of Mercy from the Northern Province, is the Head of the Religious Education Department at Thornhill College, Derry.*

Standing at the Cross-roads

Richard Collins

When I was asked to write this small personal piece, I was taken back to the time when I was part of an effort to bring the Anne Frank exhibition to Omagh. I had been studying the Holocaust and other related subjects for nearly twenty years and had often come into contact with various organizations and educational bodies. A single telephone call in mid-1995 to the Anne Frank Educational Trust in London, inquiring about the release date for Jon Blair's Oscar winning documentary, *Anne Frank Remembered* led to a casual conversation about a new, forthcoming exhibition, *Anne Frank: A History for Today*. As the conversation came to an end, my telephone friend suggested that Omagh might be a potential venue for the exhibition. "Why," I asked, "would such an important exhibition want to come to a small provincial town in Northern Ireland?" Her reply was, "And why not?"

The seed was sown, and with the full backing of Omagh's Local District Council and the Western Education and Library Board, the exhibition was booked. By the time of the official opening, ten months later, I was filled with eager anticipation. Still, an anxiety gnawed at me: What if no one showed up?

During the opening ceremony for the Anne Frank exhibit, Helen Lewis was to speak, and speak she did! Helen is a Jewish survivor of

Theresienstadt, Auschwitz, and Stutthof concentration camps. Born in Czechoslovakia, she lives now in Belfast. True perspective is a quality attained through experience and this was amply portrayed by her remarkable story of survival. Having read Helen's extraordinary book, *A Time to Speak* (Blackstaff Press, 1992), I had a mental picture of those dark times but hearing her speak, watching her body movements, and seeing her facial expressions gave a much sharper image to her story. This made me ask myself, what if Anne Frank had survived? Would her diary be what it is today? If so, what additional impact would she bring to such a gathering?

These subjective thoughts obviously have no answer, but it did occur to me that if I could be inspired to study and question the life and death of one young Jewish girl by the experience of viewing the Anne Frank exhibition, then others also could be so inspired.

Within four days of the exhibition's opening, every available time slot for school visits was booked, thus making the event, on a purely educational level, an outstanding success. Indeed, by the end of the exhibition run, the numbers of public visitors exceeded my expectations, allowing me later to reflect that Omagh, indeed, had been a wise choice for this multifaceted international exhibition. How ironic, then, that destiny marked our dear little town on the world map for the saddest of all reasons.

Images of death and despair, whether written or captured on film, are often for dramatic effect portrayed or televised in slow motion. Whilst altering and perhaps influencing an image, it is vitally important, in the name of education, that people experience, through whatever medium is available, as much detail as possible in order to comprehend an event that sometimes passes in a split second.

Omagh, Saturday, 15th August 1998: As we stood at the crossroads between Upper and Lower Market Street, amidst bodies and rubble, scanning the immediate area for a recognizable piece of our children's clothing, my wife and I watched as a fireman walked towards us carrying the lifeless body of young boy cradled in his arms. As parents, we could never have imagined such a moment. The image before us appeared to be in slow motion. To see a child killed like this, to have the fear of our own children's fate eat into our very hearts – this was truly a life-defining moment.

There were other scenes we experienced in the next hour and a half that day, until we found our children in the local hospital. These, too, appeared to us as if in slow motion. Translating those experiences now, several months later, we both feel that the images and events of August 15th, 1998 were so alien to our every day life that they seem unreal and could not possibly have taken place. But we know they did.

By late 1944, Anne Frank had been living in an unreal world for two years – a world of perpetual slow motion. Unlike our children who survived their ordeal with relatively light injuries, Anne was to perish, just like the little boy in the fireman's arms. We have a visual record of the events in Omagh. As for Anne, all we have is her Diary, and even that ends before the full horror of the Holocaust envelops her, most of her family, and their companions in the Secret Annex.

Children, like adults, live with the constant threat of violence. The arbitrary nature of violence in Northern Ireland has lasted more than twice as long as the sustained and directed terror of the Nazi period. In the main, its effects have been experienced by children through the media and television more than in person. Indeed, my own experiences until recently were of this nature, and I have lived here all my life. In saying this, of course, the impact on my life of images from "the troubles" have shaped my character in immeasurable ways. Here perhaps lies the parallel of Anne Frank's life with ours. So many of us in Northern Ireland have felt trapped and isolated by violence, and yet, we survive and develop, with hopes and aspirations which at times appear so far away.

The Holocaust is an important subject for education and must never be understated. It did happen, and in a sadly predicable way has been mirrored in other parts of the world since the end of World War II. To paraphrase, "the failure to understand and learn from the lessons of history will invariably doom one or all to repeat them." During WW II and the Holocaust, Auschwitz and Bergen Belsen were different from each other in terms of location and function, but, in the final analysis, they became exactly the same thing: places of horror and death for the Jews and other victims of the Nazis.

The understanding of history shapes the future of us all. Therefore, it is essential that whatever history is taught is both accurate and thought provoking to young people, who, after all, carry the reins of our future. Through the exhibition, *Anne Frank: A History for Today*, we can learn the lessons of how, under unimaginable circumstances, human beings can reduce themselves and others to the lowest forms of existence.

At some stage throughout our individual lives, many of us come to terms with the concept of *failure to fulfil* – others, as the result of circumstances, are never even given the opportunity to *fail to fulfil*. Through Anne Frank's story, we can draw strength from the fact that her childhood was a joyous period and even though her forced captivity was stifling and tragic, she, nevertheless, possessed an ability to dream and plan for the future. The very real threat of death during her daily existence in the Secret Annex did not prevent her from developing her true character, that of someone with dreams to fulfil.

Richard Collins, *a 1986 graduate of Heriot-Watt University in Edinburgh, Scotland, is an architect who lives in Omagh, Northern Ireland, with his wife, Noreen and their two daughters.*

Part Three

ANNE FRANK IN THE CLASSROOM

Why Holocaust Studies?

G. Jan Colijn

This essay is adapted from a September 1998 Lecture given to the inaugural class of The Richard Stockton College of New Jersey's M.A. program in Holocaust and Genocide Studies.

The Holocaust is one of the defining paradigms of the 20th century. Steven Katz, the author of *The Holocaust in Historical Context*, put it very precisely in an article in *The New York Times*: "... the distinctive features of modernity," he said, "nationalism, the decline of religious authority, an innovative political ideology, bureaucracy, technology, the secular state, racial theory, and international state-sponsored genocide – come together in a unique way."[1]

Some would say, "Fine. These elements can be studied through the disciplinary lens of different fields, such as political science, sociology, bioethics, and German history, to name a few. We don't need a whole field devoted to the subject." The problem is that the topography of this subject is too complex for one discipline. No one discipline has the answers. The questions raised by the subject are too intractably wide to address them, one discipline at a time.

But there also is another reason. The American journalist Walter Lippmann once said that education is civilisation's court of last resort. That does not mean that education provides protection against genocide. On the contrary. Many of the leading perpetrators of the Holocaust had advanced degrees, just as many of those who caused the Killing Fields in Cambodia were educated at the Sorbonne, and similarly educated were many leaders in the Rwandan massacres of 1994. Today, educated men and women, intellectuals even, play a major role in rekindling the murderous nationalisms engulfing the Balkans. James Bernauer once made the sobering comment that what is "so chilling [is] that the maps of night – Auschwitz, Dachau, Buchenwald, Mauthausen, and the other graveyards – were drawn in part by the moods, ideas and plans which grew in a supposed terrain of day and light – that extraordinary and proud Kingdom of German Universities ... Berlin, Munich, Frankfurt, Tuebingen, Freiburg."[2]

The second reason, then, is simply this: in the shadow of Auschwitz, we can no longer afford a morally bankrupt education. Education – educators – will have to centrally address the questions: What went wrong in German education in the 1920s and 30s? What continues to go wrong in education in many parts of the world today? What can we do about it?

How often we have heard the phrase "Never again!" After Cambodia, Bosnia, and Rwanda, how hollow, how utterly empty that phrase sounds today. It would give us some breathing space in human history if we could say, with *any* degree of confidence, that the Holocaust was a terrible event, but a unique one, an aberration.

If that were so, we would commemorate the victims. But from a unique event in history, nothing is to be learned. There are many, many unique aspects to the Holocaust, but it was not a unique event. It is, in Franklin Littell's felicitous phrase, the plumb line of twentieth century genocide, but genocidal attacks on minorities have continued in its wake.

In saying that the Holocaust is not unique, I do not mean here the widespread attempts to capture the power of the word "Holocaust" to describe other human calamities that deserve our serious attention, but are not genocidal in the sense of literally intending to wipe out entire peoples. I also do not mean to fall into the associated trap of analysing comparative suffering. Democide, as Rudy Rummel calls it, the mass slaughter of subjects by governments, has reached a death toll of more than 150 million in this century alone. That very fact urges us on to study the Holocaust and other genocides, to explain, to understand, in so far as we can, so that eventually we will be equipped to teach and, yes, to prevent such things from repeatedly happening in our fragile world.

In sum, there are urgent reasons for a deliberate, organized, multidisciplinary approach to these most vexing problems. They raise extraordinary analytical and moral challenges, and we look to teachers and clergy, to parents and politicians to be the frontline of our obligation to deal with these matters, as intellectuals, as human beings, and as citizens of countries that mandate compulsory education.

Teaching about the Holocaust and genocide is not easy. The issues often perplex and always abhor, but nothing you will study in the future will ever be marginal, ever seem of only peripheral importance. Everything you will study will be connected, not only with that defining paradigm of our life's century, but as you will discover, with just about anything else – bioethics, public policy, discrimination, racism, eugenics, violence, economics, nationalism, immigration, education.

And we must deal with the whole overhang of a rich, centuries old Jewish civilization in Europe, with its many triumphs, and not just with its victimhood. In addition, you will encounter examples of uncommon goodness and courage, those "righteous" Christians, and others, whose personal stories inspire us because, against all odds and against a backdrop of dehumanizing terrors, they remembered that to be human means to act on behalf of others whose lives are in danger.

Teaching about the Holocaust and genocide may confound you, perplex you, even bring you to the edge of despair, but a few years from now you will have a better, clearer road map of life itself. It may not be rosier, although as I just noted, there will be many elements to uplift and sustain you, but it will be a better map. Hence, like Aristotle before you, you will have a clearer vision as a human being, and as a teacher. Everyone who is touched by the Holocaust is a changed person. It will be up to you to give depth and meaning to that change, for yourself, for your families, and for your charges in your educational or other professional environment.

Notes

1. *The New York Times,* August 8, 1998.

2. See James Bernauer, "Our Dnagerous Moral Selves: On Nazism's spiritual-erotic reduction and the Emergence of the Holocaust Bystander," in Stephen Feinstein, et. al., eds., *Confronting the Holocaust, A Mandate for the 21st Century – Part Two,* Studies in the Shoah, vol. XX, Lanham, MD: University Press of America, 1998, pp. 55-70; 56.

G. Jan Colijn, *a Dutch national, is Dean of General Studies at The Richard Stockton College of New Jersey, USA.*

Anne Frank in the Classroom

Leo Lieberman

Anne Frank, a Dutch teenager, became famous posthumously for her diary-journal written in an Amsterdam attic while hiding from the Nazis with her family and four other Jews. Discovered after Anne died in the Bergen-Belsen concentration camp, the diary has been published in numerous languages, produced as a play on most of the world's leading stages, and made into a popular motion picture. In both its written and dramatic form Anne Frank's diary-journal is cherished for its poignancy, psychological insight, and literary talent. Written between June 14, 1942, and August 1, 1944, the diary records in unpretentious yet beautiful language the reactions of each of the members of the trapped group. The young girl's optimism, yearning for freedom, and love of others has had so deep an emotional impact on millions of people that Anne Frank has become a symbol of the wonderful Jewish children the world lost in the Holocaust.

It is, therefore, no wonder that this book and the story of this young girl who started writing her diary when she was not yet fourteen years of age has caught the imagination and has had a profound impact on adolescent boys and girls. As a result, teachers have latched onto this book as a vehicle for teaching the Holocaust to primary, secondary and grammar school students.

There are a number of excellent strategies that can be used in conjunction with teaching this important piece of literature which often serves as the heart of a unit on the Holocaust. Teenagers can be told to keep a diary or journal of their life for two or three days and then discuss the value of keeping such a record. Students often point out that a diary-journal may well act as an emotional catharsis as well as a record of their activities. And, of course, it must be pointed out that our students are writing in the security of a free and permissive society, often within the parameters of a supportive family. Their emotional and psychological drives are quite different from those of Anne's. And yet when they read the diary of this beleaguered young adolescent, they may find striking similarities in the feelings that they have and that this young Jewish girl, living in another time and in another place under difficult circumstances, possessed. They can identify with the emerging adolescent who wrote, "All the bickering, tears, and nervous tension have become such a stress and strain that I fall into my bed at night crying and thanking my lucky stars that I have half an hour to myself" (October 29, 1943).

Grammar and secondary school girls can use the Diary as a springboard to discuss the changing role of the young woman in society. (Boys, too, could benefit from such an exploration.) In June 1944, shortly after Anne turned fifteen, she recorded in her Diary, "One of the many questions that has often bothered me is why women have been, and still are thought to be, so inferior to men. It's easy to say it's unfair, but that's not enough for me; I'd really like to know the reason for this great injustice!" Students should compare the thinking of the 1940s and that of today. How far have we come? Was Anne a feminist or simply a typical young woman? Do we share these thoughts today or are they outmoded?

The concept of stereotyping is one that might well be examined in a classroom environment dedicated to teaching ethical and moral values. Students might create their own definitions of a stereotype, discuss how stereotyping, discrimination, and bigotry lead to racism and dehumanization, and how this process was part of Anne's world. The entry of May 22, 1944, might well be discussed, "Oh it's sad, very sad that the old adage has been confirmed for the umpteenth time: 'What one Christian does is his own responsibility, what one Jew does reflects on all Jews.'" The teacher should couple this entry with the response that Otto Frank, Anne's father, gave after World War II had come to an end. He responded to remarks that were made about "those Germans" by saying "which German?" He did not want to fall into the act of stereotyping by lumping all Germans together. Students should analyse both comments, that of Anne and that of Otto Frank, to see how they relate to their own lives and their own society.

In addition to teacher-selected excerpts from Anne Frank's diary-journal, students should be encouraged to pick out relevant entries for discussion and analysis. And through this analysis the teacher could serve as a guide to point out the historical context of the work. Students can benefit from working in groups. One group can research the story of the Frank family from the time that they moved from Germany to Amsterdam, Holland, a country long regarded as a safe-haven for religious groups, to May, 1940, when Germany invaded Holland and the Franks were forced to live under Nazi rule. They also could research 1942, the year the Franks went into hiding in the secret Annex above Otto Frank's office. And finally, they could delve into the months after the Annex was discovered by the Nazis and the family were taken away and sent to concentration camps, where Anne, barely 15, contracted typhus and succumbed to the disease, dying in March, 1945, just weeks before the end of WW II. Another group could concentrate on the Holocaust in Holland and cull from the Diary meaningful excerpts, such as the one from November 19, 1942, "I often see long lines of good innocent people accompanied by crying children . . . ." And a third group could develop a timeline of Anne Frank's life, beginning in May, 1925, when her parents were married, and concluding in August, 1980, with the death of Otto Frank in Switzerland. All groups should have the opportunity to share their research with the entire class.

Another valuable teaching tool is the development of a dictionary of terms related to the study of Anne Frank and the Holocaust. Such entries as *Aryan, Concentration Camps, Death Camps, Final Solution, and Yellow Star* as well as other entries suggested by students should be part of this class effort.

Finally, students should be encouraged to use the Diary as a springboard for further reading. Younger children (ten and up) could be encouraged to read such books as Inge Auerbacher's *I am a Star*, or Clara and Joan Grossman's *Clara's Story*, or even Susan Bachrach's *Tell Them We Remember: The Story of the Holocaust*. Older adolescents could go on to Ruth Sender's *The Cage*, Sonia Weitz's *I Promised I Would Tell*, and Carol Rittner's *The Courage to Care*. Reading could be supplemented by class viewing of such films as *Dear Kitty*, or *Just a Diary* (Anne Frank Centre USA), and *Daniel's Story* (U.S. Holocaust Memorial Museum).

There is no limit to what the resourceful teacher can do with such a rich and important work as *The Diary of Anne Frank*. From class illustrations to posters, from poetry writing to dramatizations, from creative interviews to research essays – all this can enrich the life experience of students at various grade levels in school. Such units can give meaning, hope and increased understanding to the words Anne Frank wrote, the words of a young girl whose life was cut short by an unfathomable evil, "I still believe, in spite of everything, that people are truly good at heart."

Leo Lieberman *is Associate Professor of Holocaust Studies at The Richard Stockton College of New Jersey, USA.*

Lesson Ongoing!

Mary Murphy

We were exploring *The Merchant of Venice* together, a group of 15 year old literature students and I. A long hard look at the Christians in the play drove us to the conclusion that, in general, they were a thoroughly unattractive bunch: variously prodigal, vulgar, irresponsible, deceptive and, to a man, vigorously anti-Semitic.

All this, and not a word of censure for their nasty ways, we noted. But then the play has a ready-made villain, doesn't it? The Jew. A dark, brooding, grasping, murderously Christian-hating fellow who cares more for his ducats than for his daughter. She, incidently is romantically involved with a nice Christian boy who is even willing to marry her, with the tiny proviso that she turn her back on her family, her race, her religion -oh, and another small thing: that she come to him furnished with money and jewels stolen from her father!

In his play, was Shakespeare slyly holding up a mirror in which his contemporaries might see reflected their anti-Semitism? Or was he a fully paid-up member of a racist, bigoted society, sharing their hatreds unthinkingly? The Jury is still out.

We talked of the invidious art of stereotyping in relation to the play and, in a related exercise, to our own society here in Northern Ireland. We agreed that to stereotype groups of people rendered them very easy to deal with:

"All Catholics are . . . ."

" All Protestants are . . . ."

Individuality is wiped out by the stereotype. No changes in mind or heart are needed. The stereotype is all. It's so easy! "Stereotyping probably led to the Holocaust," one student offered. "I mean, it probably caused the hatred which lead to the Holocaust. How else, unless the Germans suddenly turned into monsters overnight, could they bring themselves to murder millions of Jews?"

"They didn't need to turn into monsters overnight," said another student, "they had a ready-made monster: the Jewish race. They became the "good guys" - ridding the world of a monster. They became monster- slayers; heroes! Well, in their own eyes, at any rate."

And back in Northern Ireland: Recognitions. Comparisons. Epiphanies. The lesson is ongoing.

Four students opted to re-read *The Diary of Anne Frank*. Why? "Because Anne Frank is real. Nobody 'made her up.' Her feelings are real. And her experiences are real," they said.

Below are some student comments written after they had read, or re-read Anne's Diary.

The entire time Anne and her family remained in hiding, she never gave up hope. There were times when she began to falter but they talked a lot about "after the war" and her ambition to be a writer. Amazingly, Anne didn't seem to really loathe or hate the Nazis.

This quite reminded me of people living in Northern Ireland. Instead of fighting those who oppose or maybe even hate them, they just get on with their lives. Many have the attitude, "fighting and hatred will get us nowhere." Their faith in God strengthens them and gives them the ability to tolerate those who oppose them.

Despite the fact that she was living in captivity, Anne experienced the pain and troubles of teenagers everywhere. Many times it seemed that her parents favoured Margot over her, and disapproved of her special friendship with Peter. At times, we also feel as though we don't meet our parents expectations.

Maeve

Anne Frank's Diary makes us realise that no matter what tragic circumstances we are thrown into, there is always room for hope. Anne had to deal with the burden of growing, of changing, of discovering who she was. Anne's writing was never filled with depression and despair, as I think my own might have been. In her writing, we see her transcend the situation. In my opinion Anne Frank is a role model for today, both for girls and boys.

Michelle

Troubles in Northern Ireland shouldn't prevent people from following their dreams and being who they want to be. Anne's dream was to be a famous writer and, against all odds and barriers, her dream came true.

For most of us, becoming a teenager is stressful, but for Anne, it was even worse. She had no space, privacy or time to herself; she couldn't walk around the house and calm herself down after an epic battle. Our problems seem trivial compared to hers.

Despite being physically trapped in the "Secret Annex," she was mentally free, growing and maturing faster that ever in her life. She didn't let others stop her from dreaming and thinking.

Lucy

Anne Frank is an inspiration. She was independent and strong willed. In the midst of everything, the fears and tensions of being caught, Anne found love in Peter. We in Northern Ireland can learn one important element from Anne's Diary: the gift of tolerance.

Maeve

Mary Murphy, *Head of the English Department at Thornhill College in Derry, Northern Ireland, is a well-known "Thought for the Day" contributor on BBC-Radio Ulster.*

Anne Frank: A History for Today

Mary Johnson

The exhibition, *Anne Frank: A History for Today* relates the story of Anne Frank, using family photographs and passages from her Diary. Enriching Anne's own story are testimonies of her Jewish and non-Jewish contemporaries as well as historical information about the era in which she lived and died. The photos and documents portray a complex young woman living through an era when racism and discrimination culminated in the Nazi Final Solution of the Jewish people.

Racism and discrimination have persisted in the post-Auschwitz decades and have precipitated recent genocides. The exhibition emphasizes how important it is that present and future societies detect early warning signs of hatred and intolerance and seek to establish a civil society based on tolerance and mutual respect for human rights.

The central vision of the National Socialist Party [Nazis] that came to power in Germany shortly after Anne's birth was to create a perfect biological society. According to the Nazi world view, so-called "Aryans" were the perfect people whose physical and moral qualities surpassed those of non-Aryan peoples. The Jews were viewed as principal threats to the Aryan dominance. Also threatening German racial purity were the Gypsies, the physically and mentally handicapped, Slavs, and Blacks, among others. In addition to the biological enemies of the National Socialist state, there also were political and religious dissidents who refused to succumb to Nazi totalitarianism.

As unfolded in the exhibition, the years of Anne's life, 1929-1945, span the years the Nazis came to power and extended their hegemony over much of Western and Eastern Europe. Anne and her sister Margot died in the German concentration camp of Bergen Belsen just weeks before Nazi Germany surrendered in May 1945.

Although Anne's Diary ended while the inhabitants were still in the Secret Annex, the exhibition, *Anne Frank: A History for Today* follows the stories of the Franks, the Von Pels and Mr. Pfeffer in the closing months of World War II and the Holocaust. After his liberation from Auschwitz, Otto Frank, Anne's father, made his way back to Amsterdam. Miep Gies, one of the people who helped the "Secret Annexers" during their more than two years in hiding, found Anne's Diary after their arrest. She turned it over to Mr. Frank, after they learned that Anne, Margot, and Edith Otto had died in the camps.

Otto devoted the rest of his life to making Anne's Diary known to the world. He hoped her words would heighten public awareness of the dangers inherent in racism and discrimination and would inspire people to build a world based on understanding and peace. Closing panels in the exhibition showing scenes of neo-Nazi activities and "ethnic cleansing" in the former Yugoslavia suggest the work that still needs to be done to realize Mr. Frank's dream.

The exhibition expands on the traditional portrayal of Anne as a young woman who believed that all would turn out for the better despite the misery of her immediate circumstances in the Annex. Revealing the complexity of Anne's personality and the far reaching implications of the Holocaust for all minorities in Nazi Germany, the exhibition compels us to consider how difficult it is to create and maintain a pluralistic and democratic society which preserves freedom and human rights. As Vaclav Havel, President of the Czech Republic, says, "The content of Anne Frank's legacy is still very much alive and it can address us fully, especially at a time when the map of the world is changing and when dark passions are awakening within people."

After viewing the exhibition, teachers could discuss questions such as the following with their students:

- How did people allow a brutal regime like Nazism to gain ascendance in a highly educated and cultured society like Germany? Studying the photographs of crowds saluting the Nazi leadership and worshipping the Fuhrer, teachers could discuss with students why so many Germans and Europeans outside Germany saw Hitler as a saviour.

- Otto Frank is quoted in the exhibition as saying: "The world around me collapsed. I had to face the consequences, and though this did hurt me deeply I realised that Germany was not the world and I left forever." From information in the exhibition, what were some of the early signs that Nazi Germany was unsafe for Jews, even Jews who had lived in and loved Germany for centuries?

- Discuss how the Nazi concept of a racial state differs from the ideal of a democracy.

- Otto Treumann, a Jewish contemporary of Anne's, exclaimed how German nationalism "took hold of you whether you liked it or not." Discuss how a person could scapegoat others as the result of Nazi propaganda, then become swept up in the nationalistic fervour.

- Beneath the photo of Hans Massaquoi is his memory, "I was six years old when I started school in 1932. [I was persecuted by teachers and students who favoured the Nazis] One time – I must have been around ten – one of the teachers took me aside and said, 'When we've settled the score with the Jews, you'll be next.'" How did the Nazi ideal of a racial state affect all non-aryan minorities in the Third Reich?

- Why do school children everywhere read Anne Frank's Diary or the play based on Anne's Diary? Why has Anne Frank become a universal symbol for hope and tolerance?

Mary Johnson, a historian, is a Programme Associate with the well-known American educational foundation, Facing History & Ourselves, Brookline, Massachusetts, USA.

RESOURCES
FOR TEACHING

Resources For Teaching

Bibliography

Anne Frank: A History for Today. Amsterdam: Anne Frank House, 1998.
Charles, Michael J. H. *History: Europe of the Dictators, 1914-1945.* Oxfordshire, 1998, rev.
Doorly, Mary Rose. *Hidden Memories: The Personal Recollections of Survivors and Witnesses to the Holocaust Living in Ireland.* Dublin, Ireland: Blackwater Press, 1994.
Frank, Anne. B.M. Mooyart translator. *Anne Frank: The Diary of a Young Girl.* New York: Bantam Books, 1993.
Frank, Anne. Otto Frank and Mirjam Pressler eds. *The Diary of a Young Girl: The Definitive Edition.* New York: Doubleday, 1995.
Frank, Anne. David Barnouw and Gerrold Van Der Stroom. Arnold J. Pomerans translator. *The Diary of Anne Frank: The Critical Edition.* New York: Doubleday, 1989.
Gies, Miep and Alison L. Gold. *Anne Frank Remembered: The Story of the Woman Who Helped Hide the Frank Family.* Boston: G.K. Hall, 1998.
Kopf, Hedda Rosner. *Understanding Anne Frank's The Diary of a Young Girl: A Student Casebook to Issues, Sources, and Historical Documents.* Westport, CT: Greenwood Publishing Group, 1997.
Landau, Ronnie S. *The Nazi Holocaust.* London: I. B. Tauris & Co. Ltd, 1992.
Moore, Bob. *Victims & Survivors: The Nazi Persecution of the Jews in the Netherlands 1940-1945.* London: Arnold, 1997.
Muller, Melissa. *Anne Frank: The Biography.* New York: Metropolitan Books, 1998.
Rittner, Carol, ed. *Anne Frank in the World: Essays and Reflections.* New York: M.E. Sharpe, 1997.
The Holocaust Educational Trust and the Spiro Institute. *Lessons of the Holocaust.* London, 1998.

Videography

The Attic: The Hiding of Anne Frank - Yorkshire Television Enterprises, 1988.
Anne Frank: A Legacy for Our Time - Society for Visual Education, 1985.
Anne Frank Remembered – Jon Blair Film Company, Ltd., 1995.

Resources for Teaching

A Book of Dreams – Anne Frank House Amsterdam.
Eyewitness – Anne Frank House Amsterdam, 1998.
Forget Me Not: The Anne Frank Story – Grace Products Corporation, 1996.
Anne Frank: The Missing Pages – Kurtis Productions, 1998.
The Man Who Hid Anne Frank. Canada: Canadian Broadcasting System.
Understanding the Holocaust. London: Holocaust Educational Trust
    & Spiro Institute for the Study of Jewish History and Culture, 1998.

Online Resources

Anne Frank Centre USA – *http://www.annefrank.com/afc/afc.html*
The Anne Frank House – *http://www.channels.nl/amsterdam/annefran/html*
Anne Frank Online – *http://www.annefrank.com*
Anne Frank Educational Trust UK – *http://www.afet.org.uk/*
Cybrary of the Holocaust – *http://remember.org*
Holocaust Teacher Resource Centre – *http://www.holocaust-trc.org/*
The Nizkor Project – *http://nizkor.org*
Simon Wiesenthal Centre – *http://www.wiesenthal.com*
The United States Holocaust Memorial Museum – *http://www.ushmm.org*
The Virtual Anne Frank House – *http://qumran.com/anne_frank/*